D1712480

DISCARDED

DISCARDED

21st Century Junior Library

WORKING AT A RESTAURANT

by Katie Marsico

CHERRY LAKE PUBLISHING * ANN ARBOR, MICHIGAN

Published in the United States of America by Cherry Lake Publishing
Ann Arbor, Michigan
www.cherrylakepublishing.com

Content Adviser: Sharon Castle, PhD, Associate Professor of Elementary Social Studies,
George Mason University, Fairfax, Virginia

Reading Consultant: Cecilia Minden-Cupp, PhD, Literacy Specialist and Author

Photo Credits: Page 4, ©iStockphoto.com/genekrebs; page 6, ©Dinodia Images/Alamy; cover and
page 8, ©Khoo Si Lin, used under license from Shutterstock, Inc.; cover and page 10, ©VR Photos,
used under license from Shutterstock, Inc.; cover and page 12, ©iStockphoto.com/Imageegaml; page
14, ©Galina Barskaya, used under license from Shutterstock, Inc.; page 16, ©Olaf Doering/Alamy;
cover and page 18, ©Rob Marmion, used under license from Shutterstock, Inc.; page 20, ©mylife
photos/Alamy

Copyright ©2009 by Cherry Lake Publishing
All rights reserved. No part of this book may be reproduced or utilized in
any form or by any means without written permission from the publisher.

LIBRARY OF CONGRESS CATALOGING-IN-PUBLICATION DATA
Marsico, Katie, 1980–
Working at a restaurant / by Katie Marsico.
    p. cm.
Includes index.
ISBN-13: 978-1-60279-269-2
ISBN-10: 1-60279-269-0
1. Restaurants—Juvenile literature. 2. Restaurants—Employees—Juvenile
literature. I. Title.
TX945.M395 2009
647.95—dc22   2008006751

Cherry Lake Publishing would like to acknowledge the work of
The Partnership for 21st Century Skills.
Please visit www.21stcenturyskills.org *for more information.*

CONTENTS

5 What Is a Restaurant?

9 Restaurant Workers

19 Do You Want to Work at a Restaurant?

22 Glossary

23 Find Out More

24 Index

24 About the Author

Pizza is just one kind of food you can eat
at a restaurant.

What Is a Restaurant?

Can you smell the pizza? Does it make your mouth water? You are hungry! You look around the **restaurant**. There are many people who work there. You see your **waiter**. He is carrying a pizza. It is finally time to eat!

Some restaurants are open for breakfast, lunch, and dinner.

A restaurant is where people sometimes go to eat a meal. Have you ever eaten in a restaurant? There are many different jobs in restaurants. Everyone works together so you can enjoy your meal. Let's take a look at some restaurant workers.

Make a Guess!

Guess how many people work in your favorite restaurant. Write down your guess. Take your guess with you next time you go. Ask one of the workers for the exact number. Was your guess correct?

The host will take you to your table at a restaurant.

Restaurant Workers

A worker called a **host** greets you when you walk in the door. He will show you where to sit. Do you prefer a table or a booth? Maybe you want a table by the window. Just tell the host. He will do his best to place you wherever you want to be seated.

Some restaurants have more than one cook. The chef is in charge of all the cooks in the kitchen.

Who tells the workers in the kitchen what you want to eat? Waiters take your order. They bring your food to the table. These workers make sure you have everything you need to enjoy your meal.

The **chef** is in charge of the kitchen. He prepares the food. He helps the manager decide what foods **customers** might like to eat. The chef may be in charge of other cooks in the kitchen.

A busser takes away the dirty dishes when you finish eating.

Waiters could not do their job without **bussers**. A busser sets the table. He clears the dishes when you finish your meal. Bussers are one of the reasons eating at a restaurant is so fun. You do not have to clean up when you are done!

A boy reads a menu at a restaurant. A restaurant manager helps the chef plan the menu.

A **manager** runs the restaurant. She has many important jobs. The manager hires the other workers. She also plans the **menu** with the chef. She orders supplies such as food and napkins.

Have you ever told a restaurant manager that you liked your meal? The manager listens to what customers have to say. She wants you to come back and eat at her restaurant again.

An inspector checks a restaurant kitchen. He wants to make sure it is clean and safe.

Restaurant managers work closely with **inspectors**. An inspector makes sure everything in a restaurant is clean and safe. He watches how workers handle food. Do they wash their hands often? An inspector helps keep the restaurant a nice place to visit.

What is the difference between a **cafeteria** and a restaurant? Hint: who carries your food to your table at school?

A cafeteria has no hosts or waiters. School cafeterias do not have bussers to clean tables. Cafeterias do have people who cook food and wash dishes.

Do you like to help prepare meals at home?

Do You Want to Work in a Restaurant?

Would you like to work in a restaurant one day? It is not too early to start planning ahead! Talk to workers when you visit a restaurant. Find out how they **trained** for this kind of work.

Many people enjoy working with food. Do you like cooking? Ask the adults in your family if you can help plan and cook meals.

19

Restaurant workers must clean up after cooking meals. You can practice by washing dishes at home.

Setting and clearing the table will help you get ready for a job in a restaurant. So will washing the dishes.

A restaurant can be a great place to work. Learn as much as you can now. Then you can decide if one of the jobs you have just read about is right for you!

GLOSSARY

bussers (BUHSS-uhrz) workers who help waiters and waitresses by setting and clearing tables

cafeteria (kaf-uh-TIHR-ee-uh) a restaurant where people get their own food and bring it back to their tables

chef (SHEFF) a skilled cook who is often in charge of other cooks in a kitchen

customers (KUHSS-tum-uhrz) people who visit a business, such as a restaurant, to buy something or use a service

host (HOHST) a person who greets people at a restaurant and shows them to their tables

inspectors (in-SPEK-tuhrz) workers who check restaurants to make sure they are safe and clean

manager (MAH-ni-jer) someone who is usually in charge of all the other workers

menu (MEN-yoo) a list of all the foods that can be ordered in a restaurant

restaurant (RESS-tuh-rahnt) a place where people pay to eat meals prepared by other people

trained (TRAYND) to be taught a skill

waiter (WAY-tur) someone who serves people food and drinks in a restaurant

FIND OUT MORE

BOOKS

Dunn, Mary. R. *I Want to Be a Chef*. New York: PowerKids Press, 2009.

Kishel, Ann-Marie. *Server*. Minneapolis: LernerClassroom, 2007.

WEB SITES

The Culinary Institute of America—Planning to Be a Chef
www.ciakids.com/forkids/planning.html
Read about the skills you will need to be a chef

U.S. Department of Labor and U.S. Department of Education—Career Voyages
www.careervoyages.gov/students-elementary.cfm#hospitality
Click on "Hospitality" and watch videos about different restaurant jobs

INDEX

B
booths, 9
bussers, 13, 17

C
cafeterias, 17
chefs, 11, 15
cleaning, 13, 17, 21
cooking, 11, 17, 19
cooks, 11
customers, 11, 15

D
dishes, 13, 17, 21

F
food, 11, 15, 17, 19, 21

H
hiring, 15
hosts, 9, 17

I
inspectors, 17

K
kitchens, 11, 21

M
managers, 11, 15
menus, 15, 21

S
safety, 17
seating, 9
shopping, 21

**skills, 21
supplies, 15

T
tables, 9
training, 19

W
waiters, 5, 11, 17

ABOUT THE AUTHOR

Katie Marsico is the author of more than 30 children's books. She lives in Elmhurst, Illinois, with her husband and two children. She would especially like to thank the staff at Rainbow Restaurant in Elmhurst for helping her research this title.

Working at a restaurant

33500010323947   3ae